The Bumper Book of
OPERATIC DISASTERS

The Bumper Book of

OPER TIC DIS STERS

HUGH VICKERS

Illustrated by Michael ffolkes

With an Introduction by Sir Peter Ustinov

PAN BOOKS

First published 1998 by Pan Books
an imprint of Macmillan Publishers Ltd
25 Eccleston Place, London SW1W 9NF
and Basingstoke

Associated companies throughout the world

ISBN 0 330 37305 6

A CIP catalogue record for this book is available from the British Library.

Typeset by The Florence Group, Stoodleigh, Devon
Printed and bound in Great Britain by
Mackays of Chatham plc, Chatham, Kent

I take this chance to offer a dedication to the memory of the late Sir Georg Solti. Opera in England may recover from his loss – somehow.

With all my thanks and love to Caroline Wise.

CONTENTS

INTRODUCTION

(Great Operatic Disasters, 1979)

There is no art form which attempts the sublime while defying the ridiculous with quite the foolhardiness of opera. Even without invoking disaster, there are perils when all is going well. We often have to accept, and do so willingly, that a lady lavishly endowed with substance is an object of unrequited masculine desire simply because she is equally endowed with a voice. Things are hardly helped when her paramour is revealed to be under five foot, even with built-up shoes which make his every step across a raked stage a hazard. Matters are further complicated in this day and age by the fact that most permanent operatic troupes contain four main elements with many variations and nuances in between: those who can sing but can't act, which is perhaps the classical operatic case; those who can act but who can no longer sing, and who are often tremendously effective in smaller character roles; those paragons who can both sing and act, frequently young Americans with nowhere to go but Europe; and those who can neither act nor sing, retained in harness by some humanitarian pension scheme.

The paradoxes were surely easier to accept when the operatic stage was dominated by the first two categories, but today when suddenly confronted by thin, desirable Marguerites or Toscas, or enervating voluptuous Salomes, and tall, thin Cavaradossis, Fausts and John the Baptists, the quadruple standards are pushed further apart than ever.

The consequence of all this has been the natural one of placing critics and cognoscenti in orbit in a stratosphere of refinement where the true and the absurd are often indistinguishable from one another. After all, the stupidity of a stupid man is exercised in a restricted field; the stupidity of an intelligent man has a much wider diffusion, and a far greater effect, aided as it is by the element of surprise.

Experts on wine and balletomanes, bullfighting aficionados and opera buffs have all honed their sensibilities and garlanded their vocabularies to give expression to the new subtleties of appreciation, the endless reading between invisible lines, the endless attribution of surmised intentions, the pharisaical basking in pleasures reserved for only the most exclusive ears, eyes and mouths.

Occasionally the arbiters of elegance fall out among themselves, adding to our amusement. Only the other day a distinguished critic in a great English newspaper, who shall remain nameless for the simple reason that it is not the function of those who know they are not critics to insult those who think they are by throwing their own words back at them, accorded *Nabucco* at the Paris Opéra a drubbing. This pundit accused the public of cheering its head off for half an hour (this compared unfavourably with the Swedish critic who once went out of his way to praise a performance, but had cause to end his article with the terse words 'the public failed'). In his annoyance at being outvoted, this *Feinschmecker* alleged that, despite the reign of Rolf Liebermann, the Paris public appears as provincial as it was twenty-five years ago to the outsider used to the Met. and Covent Garden, 'The difference is that it now deludes itself into believing that its taste is the height of musical sophistication.' O divine conceit! The habitués of the Met. and Covent Garden naturally believe nothing of the sort about themselves. They are above, below or beside that sort of consideration, although perhaps to a really sophisticated and knowledgeable public, like that of Osnabruck or Marseilles, Parma or Ljubljana, the nadir of provincialism may well be achieved not only in Paris, but also in New York and London.

Those who write about opera, or discuss it on radio, provide us with the smiles, the simpers and the chuckles. Now along comes Hugh Vickers with the belly-laughs, without which no consideration of the glories of opera and its attendant '*précieuses ridicules*' would be complete.

Even a superbly run establishment like the Hamburg Opera is never disaster-proof. One extra fell ill before a performance of *Gotterdammerung*, but it seemed hardly worth calling a rehearsal for his replacement. After all, the only action for Schultz was to go out with Schmidt, who had done it many times before, and they would pick up the bier with Siegfried lying on it, and carry it solemnly into the wings. All the stage manager insisted upon was that Schultz look solemn. Schmidt explained the action in cursory fashion to his colleague and both men went into the canteen to while away the time. When the moment came, Schultz and Schmidt, looking solemn as hell, marched on to the stage. Each picking up one end of the bier, they found themselves facing one another. Dropping the bier both turned outwards and lifted the bier again. Not all Wagner's genius, not all Schultz's solemnity, could prevent the stolid Hamburgers from producing a gale of laughter followed by a storm of applause. The great power and beauty of opera at its best would be lacking a dimension without a possibility of disaster, a hint of bathos. It is on a razor's edge that the finest things are invariably accomplished and it is, therefore, not an impertinence to record its disasters, but a necessary adjunct to every act of reverence.

On page 30 you will find an account of how I introduced my young daughter to opera, and with what results. I will now happily encourage her further by sending her a copy of Hugh Vickers's delightful book.

PETER USTINOV

PREFACE

I am most grateful to Macmillan for this reissue of my two Operatic Disaster Books.

Since their publication, disasters concerning opera organizations in real life have rapidly – at least in the UK – come to surpass the simple mishaps to be seen on stage. Yet the Royal Opera House, replacing its Chief Executives as often as balloons are shot out in a fairground stall, appears to enjoy the most touching loyalty from its supporters. It is their *motivation*, however, which continues to give one food for thought.

Listen to their totally surreal comments in the interval! (See p. 90.) Or even before the opera starts. Quite recently, *avant le deluge* at Covent Garden, I was queuing for matinée tickets for the excellent *Salomé* behind a couple who, with utmost concern, asked the box-office manager what time the (surely rather short) performance ended. When the reply came '6.30 or so', she immediately turned to her companion and said 'That's all right then. We'll be back home in time for *Casualty*.' It did strike me that after two and a half hours of unremitting lust, necrophilia, blasphemy and murder there must be something worryingly odd about someone who would need to see *Casualty* as well.

Another recent development is a marked increase in the physical dangers associated with performance. My unfortunate tenor in *Carmen* (p. 18) was at least only arrested by the Mexican police for pretending to be a singer, when he was plainly an army deserter. A far more alarming event occurred the other day (April 5th 1998), when the baritone Quentin Hayes, singing with the city of Birmingham Touring Opera in Janacek's *Cunning Little Vixen*, left the theatre for a moment in his costume as – can you believe it? – a National Front thug (Union Jack shirt, Doc Marten boots). Pinned against the wall by the first two black passers-by he met, how could he explain that he was no racist, but a singer impersonating one in an especially witless, misconceived, 'relevant' opera production? I bet the performance he gave, to save his life, of Figaro's *Largo al factotum* was not merely his best ever but probably the best anywhere since Mariano Sabile used to sing it in the 1930s.

I hope new readers will enjoy this little book. I'm sure the new Millennium – preceded by its already catastrophic Dome – will prove just as operatically disastrous as the last.

HUGH VICKERS
27 April 1998

PUBLISHER'S NOTE

As in the previous volumes, some of the events in this book are well documented and incontrovertibly true; others have a basis in truth but have been somewhat embellished along the way; still others are almost certainly apocryphal but, '*se non è vero, è ben trovato*'. And, once again, the author and publisher will be delighted to hear from members of the public and of the operatic trade about new disasters for future volumes.

TECHNICAL HITCHES
and PRACTICAL JOKES

Let us begin with the most famous of all disasters. Though it has a certain legendary quality it did really happen – and in fact I have run it to earth.

TOSCA *Giacomo Puccini*
City Center, New York, 1960

Whereas most such disasters depend on some element of misunderstanding and incompetence among the stage-management, this catastrophe is – delightfully – due entirely to ill will, in this case between the stage staff and the soprano. With diabolical cunning they permitted her, after several stormy rehearsals, to complete her first performance without mishap until the very last moment, when Tosca throws herself off the battlements of the Castel Sant'Angelo. What normally happens is that on her cry '*Scarpia, davanti a Dio*' she hurls herself off and lands on a mattress four feet below (who but Callas has ever looked totally convincing at that moment? – her outstretched hands haunt the memory). But in this case it was not Callas, but a large young American who landed not on a mattress, but – perish the thought – on a *trampoline*. It is said that she came up fifteen times before the curtain fell – sometimes upside down, then the right way up – now laughing in delirious glee, now screaming with rage ... Worse still, it seems that the unhappy lady was unable to reappear in any other Opera Center performance throughout the entire season because the Center's faithful audience, remembering the trampoline, would have burst into laughter. She had to remove herself to San Francisco,

where of course no such grotesque incident could possibly occur ...

TOSCA
San Francisco Opera, 1961

One must remember that *Tosca* is very often the Cinderella – the last opera of the season – in a big opera house. This is because it is thought to be an 'easy' opera; there are in effect only three principals – Tosca, Cavaradossi and Scarpia. Looked at from the point of view of an over worked producer under great pressure, 90 per cent of the battle obviously lies in the principals knowing the work – the other participants amount only to the first-act chorus (some rehearsal needed here), the second-act choir (off-stage thank God) and the third-act execution squad (no problem, they don't sing ...). Alas, it is thus that fatal errors, hideous disasters, are engendered. On this particular occasion that innocuous firing squad was composed of hurriedly enlisted and highly enthusiastic college boys from the local campus, totally ignorant of the story and constantly worrying the producer with their 'When do we come on? What do we do?' His answer was an invariable, 'Wait, wait – I'm working with the principals.' In the end, a combination of illness and a desperately tight schedule led to the cancellation of the dress rehearsal and the appearance on the opening night of the execution squad itself only five minutes after their first and only consultation with the producer. He was still in a hurry, but felt he had given them enough to go on – 'OK, boys. When the stage manager cues you, slow-march in, wait until the officer lowers his sword, then shoot.' But how do we get off?' 'Oh – well, exit with the principals.' (This is the standard American instruction for minor characters, servants etc.)

The audience, therefore, saw the following: a group of soldiers marched on to the stage but stopped dead in its tracks at the sight of *two* people, not one as they had assumed – a man and a woman, both looking extremely alarmed. When they pointed their hesitant rifles at the man, he at first drew himself up, looking noble and resigned, but then started giving inexplicable conspiratorial sidelong glances at the woman ... they pointed them at her, but she made a series of violently negative gestures – but then what else would she do if she was about to be shot? Should they, perhaps, shoot them both? But then they would hardly be standing so far apart – anyway, the opera was called *Tosca*, it was evidently tragic, the enormous woman on stage was presumably Tosca herself, solemn funereal music was playing, the officer was raising his sword ...

Thus it happened. By a perfectly sensible process of logical deduction they *shot Tosca instead of Cavaradossi*. To their amazement they then saw the man, some twenty yards away, fall lifeless to the ground, while the person they *had* shot rushed over to him crying (we must remember this was in a vivid American translation), 'Come on, baby, get up, we gotta go.' What could they do? They had shot one of the principals – though admittedly the wrong one – and their next instruction was '*Exit with the principals.*' In disbelief they watched as, first, Spoletta and his minions burst on to the stage, and Tosca – could it be true? took up her position on top of the battlements. She jumped, and there was only one thing for it – as the curtain slowly descended the whole firing squad threw themselves after her . . .

DON GIOVANNI
W. A. Mozart, Vienna State Opera, 1958

Many operas end like *Tosca* with the sudden descent of the hero to some nether realm. Don Giovanni, however (as in Zeffirelli's production for Covent Garden), tends simply to disappear amid whirling clouds of stage-smoke as the chorus of off-stage demons promise him worse torments below. In Vienna, however, Cesare Siepi ended his admirable interpretation standing on a stage lift which, as so often happens, stuck halfway down, leaving his head and shoulders visible to the audience but not the rest of him. The technicians' efforts merely revealed the operation of one of the great laws governing opera disasters – that the most that can be hoped for is to restore the status quo ante – that is, they merely brought him back up again. Siepi then amazed the public by refusing simply to walk off and with courageous professionalism challenged the lift operator to a second attempt. Of course exactly the same thing happened, and amid the shocked silence of the Staatsoper a single voice rang out – it is said in Italian – 'Oh my God, how wonderful – hell is full.'

DON GIOVANNI
City Center, New York, 1958

Here the audience had the extraordinary experience of seeing straight through the opera to the outside world. In one of the those epic accidents which haunt the dreams of stage managers by night, *all* the scenery involved in the scene-change before Don Giovanni's feast was simultaneously raised above the proscenium level at a moment when the curtains were open and the vast doors at the back of the stage were also open to admit the entry of the new set. For ten heavenly seconds, therefore, the audience saw not eighteenth-century Spain but East 55th Street – cars passing, taxis hooting, a couple of astonished traffic cops staring at them, presumably no less amazed than they – an extreme clash between reality and illusion utterly befitting New York. Indeed every city perhaps gets the disasters it deserves.

DON GIOVANNI
City Center, New York, 1960

Boats, swans, balloons, horseback – even skis: opera offers so many different ways of getting on stage, each usually more accident-prone than the last. But *nothing* is more fatal than a sedan chair. On this occasion the producer decided to give one to Donna Elvira – a grandiose entrance involving two porters carrying her up a ramp behind the scene so that she could appear from the back of the steeply raked stage; she would then step out of the chair to begin 'Ah! *chi mi dice mai*'.

Unfortunately, she weighed a great deal and the porters only just made it up the ramp. As they arrived at the top, the one in front momentarily put his burden down, thus throwing all the weight on to the one behind – he in turn threw the chair forward, and the see-saw movement caused the soprano to turn a somersault and get stuck upside down. To make it worse, the bearers had no idea of this – indeed the very point of a sedan chair is that the porters cannot see the goings-on inside it. Unaware that anything untoward had happened, they shouldered their burden and came on to the stage unable to understand the howls of joyous laughter that greeted them. I was not there myself, but Jim Reeve, who was one of the porters, swears that she did in fact sing the whole of 'Ah! *chi mi dice mai*' upside down, though he didn't himself at first realize her predicament. There was nothing for it but to let her complete the aria and then carry her off, but even then it proved impossible to extricate her from the sedan chair in the wings –

she had become *identified* with it. A distraught stage manager summoned the house firemen to smash it with their axes, and her first gesture (a fine display of traditional soprano temperament) was to slap the two completely innocent bearers across the face as hard as she could ...

RIGOLETTO
Giuseppe Verdi, L'Opéra, Paris, 1954

Of all the things that can go wrong with *Rigoletto* this is surely the worst, affecting what we might loosely describe as the emotional heart of the entire opera. At the very moment when the courtiers are brutally mocking him in Act II, Rigoletto's hump slid slowly down his back. As their taunts increased, the audience was puzzled to see a hunchback transformed before their eyes into a perfectly normal man – except for an enormous behind. Guy Parsons of Geneva, who witnessed this, assures me, however, that much more entrancing were the baritone's efforts to push the hump back up again, while singing the great cavatina beginning '*la la, la la*'. *Cortigiani, vil razza dannata*, indeed. As he points out, one would have thought they *knew* something about handling hunchbacks in Paris . . .

DON GIOVANNI
King's Theatre, Edinburgh, 1949

Fortunately it is not usually obvious to opera spectators at the Edinburgh Festival that the theatre in which they are sitting is itself a technical disaster. Naturally it is the Italian technicians who find the most difficulty – I remember the entire technical staff of the San Carlo Theatre of Naples walking out in despair after trying to set up the lighting for Cilea's *Adriana Lecouvreur* all night, only to find that on a dry Edinburgh Sunday there wasn't even a drink to be had. But even though the backstage has been greatly improved, the shallow orchestra pit continues to present an insoluble problem of balance between singers and orchestra.

The *Don Giovanni* was the Glyndebourne version but conducted by Rafael Kubelik, who became obsessed with the relationship between the Commendatore on his pedestal in the churchyard and the three trombones which accompany his pronouncements. After spending the morning trying various vantage points behind the stage the bass, David Franklin, who was hungry for lunch, facetiously suggested that he sing it from the Gents' lavatory in the passage to the greenroom. This worked so well that Kubelik, with Carl Ebert, Jani Strasser and other members of the Glyndebourne staff, insisted on the trombones playing in there with him; despite the cramped conditions out came exactly the echoing other-worldly sound required. But, alas – on the first night the unprecedented occurred – a mechanical system in the King's Theatre actually carried out its allotted task. The long-defunct automatic flush system suddenly came torrentially to life at the exact moment of '*Di rider finirai pria dell'aurora*' – and since the performance was being broadcast, BBC Third Programme listeners were deluged even more powerfully than the spectators.

Talking of the Commendatore, it seems that dressing for the part can be a far from pleasant experience. Encased in canvas robes stiffened with size to suggest the marble, one still has to undergo the ordeal of the white make-up. Franklin relates how at Glyndebourne in 1938 one of the designer's assistants started flicking blobs of yellow paint at his face. 'What's that for?' he asked as one stuck in his eye. 'Well, you're a statue, aren't you?' 'So?' 'Pigeons!'

RIGOLETTO
Royal Opera House, Covent Garden, London, 1948

Covent Garden seasons after the war seem to have produced a number of lively incidents. The orchestra's constant teasing of the somewhat over-Germanic conductor Karl Rankl reached its climax in their launching into the overture to *Carmen* at the start of the dress rehearsal of *The Magic Flute* – 'You see, it's April Fool's Day,' explained the leader – 'It was a joke ...' 'A *joke?*' Then again, we have the incident of the scene-shifters in *Die Walküre* refusing to shift the rocks – it said 'rocks' in their contract, but 'Them's not ordinary rocks, them's *Wagnerian* rocks.' Prophetic words which, one might say, launch a major *leitmotif* in post-war opera production. As for *Rigoletto* – our story concerns that admirable English tenor Walter Midgely. During '*Questa o quella*' he got the end of his moustache caught in his mouth and gradually, inexorably, sucked it in. When he finished the aria the whole thing was stuck somewhere in his windpipe, but he managed to blow it out right across the orchestra pit – by some accounts hitting Erich Kleiber in the face.

TOSCA
San Diego, 1956

This is a perfect American disaster, in that in the USA they should surely depend on the unexpected malfunctioning of supposedly infallible mechanical equipment – computerize it and it *can't* go wrong. None the less one should (as we have seen) be very careful with *Tosca* – by far the most jinxed of operas, as *Macbeth* is in the theatre. In fact, I always feel great trepidation when Tosca stabs Scarpia – blood – real blood – has been drawn on at least three known occasions, once in a 1919 Rome production under Toscanini. Passions on stage have by then run so high that it seems rather modest of Tosca merely to skewer the villainous police chief with a fruit knife; one sits back relieved to think that now all she has to do is to place the candles beside the body and blow out the candelabra on the table. There are only four candles and with modern fireproofing the fire risk is usually considered small enough to permit the use of the real thing. At San Diego, however, they were not merely electric, but the order of their going out was fixed on a computer tape along with all the rest of the lighting cues – the tape obeyed the stage manager's signal and snuffed the candles exactly as she blew them out – except that on this occasion the programming was wrong and it blew them out in a different order from hers. She blew to the right, the candle to the left went out, she blew the back one, the one in front went out – and as she began 'E avanti a lui tremava tutta Roma' the electronic bleep for the curtain arrived too soon and

15

the curtain shut with furious speed before she'd finished, only to open again for the pre-set curtain call, shutting for good at the exact moment that she and Scarpia walked forward for their applause.

A VILLAGE ROMEO AND JULIET
Frederick Delius, London, 1920

This is the beautiful Delius score, conducted on that occasion by Sir Thomas Beecham with Eugène Goossens as his somewhat inexperienced assistant. If, dear reader, your knowledge of this work is confined to its charming intermezzo, 'The Walk to the Paradise Garden', let me inform you that its last act involves descent mechanisms quite comparable to those in *Tosca* and *Don Giovanni* – in fact the lovers scuttle their boat in the middle of a lake at the end of the love duet. On this occasion, Goossens, cueing the stage management, gave the signal four pages too early and the boat sank into the lake with the lovers delivering most of the duet from under water . . . 'Very well,' snarled Sir Thomas, 'next time you can conduct it yourself.' Goossens did so, but on this occasion the cue was given four pages too late and no one was drowned at all. 'Humph – more drama in your version, I suppose.'

CARMEN
Georges Bizet, Mexico City, date unknown

This performance of *Carmen* in modern dress took place in the bullring itself. It was a hot, heavy night in Mexico City, thirsty work for any tenor, and in the interval between Acts 3 and 4 Don José, who was an imported Italian, dashed out into the neighbouring streets to buy himself a well-earned beer. The tiny *calles* near the bullring are the haunts of thieves and murderers, and he hadn't gone ten yards before he was arrested by a healthy posse of policemen and dragged off to the local station. His cries were unavailing – the officers could clearly see that the man they were arresting was a disreputable soldier, probably a deserter. When he explained in mangled Spanish that he was not a deserter but an Italian tenor singing the part of a deserter, they informed him that he was drunk. He only got out by singing '*cette fleur que tu m'avais jetée*' to his captors all over again.

ANIMALS and
other NATURAL HAZARDS

The use of horses on the operatic stage certainly goes back to the seventeenth-century Florentine masque; but I sometimes wonder if the often alarming use of animals in general may not take us back even further, to the gladiatorial contests in the Colosseum. Significantly, in 1969 a private impresario came very near to being allowed to mount a series of bullfights in the Roman Arena at Verona, between opera productions, but was prevented by the application of an obscure Fascist law originally designed for the protection of domestic pets. Unfortunately, few operas deal with persecuted Christians, though we have a fine exception in Gaetano Donizetti's *Poliuto*.

POLIUTO
Rome Opera, 1951

The climactic scene in *Poliuto* occurs when the tenor renounces his love in favour of the Christian faith. The last aria is actually sung in the arena, and the producer (Aldo Piccinato) 'yielded to pressure' (his words) and agreed to present two live lions on stage, in cages, one on each side. The reaction of the big cat family to the human voice singing above the stave had not been calculated, nor were the bars of the cages close enough together. Strangely enough the animals didn't seem to mind the soprano, but when the tenor Carlo Bini reached his top C sharp, he suddenly found his shoulder gripped by an enormous paw . . .

One of the principles which guide Italian opera producers who decide to use animals to enhance the spectacle is that to justify the expense they must appear as often as possible. Thus the laborious procession of elephants and camels in *Aida* must appear not once, but over and over again – they constitute, as it were, a dramatic statement in themselves, like the animals in *The Magic Flute*. It all takes so long – the amount of *time* occupied in *Norma* by Pollione appearing in his chariot pulled by four horses can be immense (an attempt to vary this by using four zebras in the Baths of Caracella, Rome, in 1938 was apparently not successful). One would hardly have thought, though, that *Carmen* could be even a possible candidate for such treatment. Not at all . . .

CARMEN
Verona Arena, 1970

It was horses all the way – thirty-eight horses to be exact. They crossed and recrossed the stage in the background during the first act. They turned up to take José away from the inn in the second act. The third act opened with them all standing – a rather forlorn little group – on an artificial mountain. In Act IV they reappeared for Escamillo's procession, covered in Spanish finery and ridden by the picadors, but looking alarmingly tired and nervous. In fact all went well until the very last horse made its way from the back round in a great circle to the Plaza de Toros on the right of the stage. As it approached the orchestra pit the conductor (Gianandrea Gavazzeni) gave a violent upbeat, and the horse took off towards him as if the orchestra pit was Becher's Brook. But that splendid old maestro must have worked some instant magic – the horse merely landed on the kettledrums with an enormous crash, miraculously injuring neither itself nor its rider. We waited with bated breath to see what *could* happen next – in fact it proved to be the spectacle of Gavazzeni laying down his baton (the unthinkable!) and – fatally – murmuring (forgetting that in that unique auditorium the slightest whisper is at once audible to 15,000 people) the words *'Quel piccolo finocchio di regista'* (an Italian insult better not translated).

Amid cascades of laughter the whole procession had to unwind backwards and then re-enter, this time without mishap. Judge of our amazement then, when in the last act, just as Franco Corelli was preparing to kill Grace Bumbry, a cat came bounding down from the back of the Arena (cats at Verona play much the same role as bats at Glyndebourne). Naturally attracted to whichever of the two was singing, it rubbed itself against Corelli's legs, purring and looking wistfully up as he cried *'Eh bien, damnée.'*

Of course, horses out of doors in Verona, Rome or Avignon look realistic at least, but what of a single horse on stage in a theatre? Cocteau says that a real horse on stage looks like a strange mythological beast, that to make a believable theatrical horse you would have to make a completely symbolic animal of wood and canvas. The last horse I saw on stage indoors was in *Boris Godunov*.

BORIS GODUNOV
Modest Mussorgsky, Royal Opera House, Covent Garden, London, 1958

The libretto specifies that the Pretender – Dmitri – should appear on horseback at the head of his army. On this occasion Covent Garden had obviously grasped the point that a very large Yugoslav tenor requires a very large horse; indeed I have never seen so vast an animal outside the Yorkshire hunting field. Of course no one paid any attention to the excellently sung 'Revolution' aria, so gripped were we by what the horse might or might not do – but fortunately it was as good as gold until the applause at the end of the aria, when the horse joined in by expressing itself in the only manner obviously available to it, and in very large measure. The extraordinary thing was that when Dmitri and his followers had gone off, those erratic Covent Garden follow spotlights ('Gundogs in a snipe-infested marsh' Visconti once called them) all focused on what the horse had left, while the solitary Idiot, sitting beside it, sang of the ruin of Russia . . . Indeed, no disaster, but a masterstroke of neo-Bayreuth symbolism!

GIULIETTA & ROMEO
Riccardo Zandonai, La Scala, Milan, 1913

When are we going to see this work again? It's much more exciting than Gounod's, the Bellini is too rarely given, the Berlioz is hardly an opera. In Zandonai's version Romeo gallops into exile from Verona in a snowstorm, making use of the early revolve stage, which permits a horse to gallop flat out against the stage moving at the same speed in the opposite direction. On 13 December 1913 the Scala revolve stopped in the middle of the scene and then started going forward, first unseating Romeo and then propelling his horse into the wings with the force of a rocket. Romeo was left sitting on the frantically revolving stage, a whirling, disconsolate figure, as the artificial snow kept falling.

Bernard Levin contributes this shaggy-dog story:

CARMEN
Bournemouth, date unknown

It was a Sadler's Wells tour, and they were at Bournemouth with *Carmen*. In the middle of the smuggler's scene a gigantic Pyrenean mountain dog wandered onto the stage. (Apparently, the Bournemouth theatre they were using was part of a building with offices and other rooms, and the dog, which belonged to one of the officials working there, was a very friendly beast and had the run of the building.) Many of the audience who were unfamiliar with the opera thought it was part of the scene and were delighted. (Others who knew better were doubtless even more delighted.) The dog eventually roamed downstage opposite the conductor where it became hypnotized by the baton, which by then was being used partly to conduct the music and partly to try to shoo the beast away. Unfortunately, the dog was also used to having people throw sticks for it to fetch, and was convinced that the baton was about to be thrown. When it wasn't, the dog became cross and emitted a series of mournful barks. These, when added to by the cries of 'piss off!' which the Carmen (who had been endeavouring to kick it surreptitiously to no avail) was adding to the uproar, finally persuaded those in charge to bring the curtain down. And not a moment too soon; I imagine, except for collectors of such disasters like us who could willingly have gone on for hours longer.

As a father taking his very well-brought-up young daughter to the opera for the first time, Peter Ustinov was unwise enough to choose the Baths of Caracalla in Rome. So far we have allowed the Arena at Verona to have pride of place as far as animals are concerned, and my own memories of Caracalla are virtually limited (perforce) to the constant cries of 'Gelati, gelati!' (ice cream) which obliterated the entire performance – which, incidentally, was also completely invisible from where I was. Mr Ustinov must have had a better seat, because he could actually *see* that the whole stage (this was *Aida*) became at a certain point completely *covered* with animals – camels, elephants, horses, unwanted cats, etc. At a climactic point, *all* the animals relieved themselves simultaneously. As he stared aghast at this incredible sight, he felt a light tapping on his shoulder, and his daughter's earnest voice – 'Daddy, is it all right if I laugh?'

How could I have omitted the following Beecham story?

CARMEN
Georges Bizet, Royal Opera House, Covent Garden, c. 1932

Halfway through the third act Sir Thomas became aware that a horse was present on stage, intended to add local colour to the smugglers' cave scene. It was in fact the same old cab-horse that Covent Garden always used to use as Grane in *Gotterdammerung*, beloved

by audiences for its droll habit of munching the scenery. On this occasion, however, it suddenly turned its back on the proceedings with a decisive and dramatic gesture and performed the ultimate indiscretion. The music stopped, silence fell through the theatre and from the pit came the judgment of Sir Thomas: 'A critic, by God.'

BORIS GODUNOV
Modest Mussorgski, The Bolshoi Theatre, Moscow, 1979

The Bolshoi's horse is always of exquisite musicality. A correspondent writes that he was hypnotized by the way, throughout the two arias in which the singer was actually mounted on it, it flicked its enormous ears in time to the music with the beatific smile of a Derby winner. During the applause it would paw the ground, but this was rather unfortunate since its vast hooves produced a cavernous booming sound from the stage boards, inappropriate to a location on the Russian steppes . . .

Bears

One of my correspondents writes to say how much he enjoys frequenting pubs immediately opposite stage doors, rubbing shoulders with Roman soldiers, Dukes of Mantua, bears and so on. *Bears?* This really started me thinking – in how many operas do *bears* appear? It reminded me of a conversation I had with the producer Aldo Piccinato, years ago, in which he could not remember in which opera he had used live lions. We tried a process of elimination: *Figaro?* Surely not. *The Merry Widow?* Hardly. (The answer was, of course, Donizetti's *Poliuto*.) However, the only opera I know with a singing bear in it is Renaldo da Capua's *La Zingara* (1752). This is a delectable opera buffa about a gypsy brother and sister who cheat an elderly merchant by selling him a performing bear which is in fact the brother in disguise. In producing this work I learnt a great deal (*a*) about the use of bears on stage, (*b*) about the temper of tenors forced to rehearse in a heavy bear costume in a hundred-degree heatwave, but, above all, (*c*) about the glorious intricacies of hiring a bear costume. I arrived at Theatre Zoo, Drury Lane (to whom all thanks), armed with the measurements of the tenor and asked if they had a bear costume. The assistant looked at me pityingly. 'What type of bear?' he asked. 'Well, how many types are there?' 'Well, there are three, ain't there, smooth bear, rough bear, and very rough bear.' 'Well,' I said, 'just for the hell of it, let's try very rough bear.' 'What type of head?' he asked. 'Head?' 'Yes, rigid headpiece or furry face mask?' 'Well, let's try furry face mask.' 'Colour?'

(By now I was prepared for anything.) 'Well, how many colours have you got?' 'Well, there is black, dark brown, medium brown, light brown, beige, pink-pantomime and white.'

I ended up with a wonderful shaggy dark brown creature and an auspicious, if unusual start, to the career of the young tenor Adrian Martin.

Florence

It appears that the baritone Gratarollo was forced throughout the entire season into some form of absurd rivalry with a *seal* in the local zoo. The animal cried out in delirious joy whenever he hit a high note. This suggests that zoos and opera houses should not be placed close together . . .

The story suggests, not for the first time, that all opera depends essentially on the physical effect of the voice, whether it be human, animal or even something between the two . . . For centuries the most admired operatic voice was the castrato. It is an authenticated fact that many boy singers preferred to undergo the operation rather than lose their voices, in the full knowledge of everything this choice would entail. Perhaps some of the desperate modern passion for our singers – Callas, Sutherland – does try to resurrect a similar absolute belief in art – if you like the frightening intensity which made *Cavalleria Rusticana* and *I Pagliacci* eliminate all rivals on the stage, if you like that element in opera which can only be called aggressive, an assault on the emotions.

Eighteenth-century accounts constantly refer to formal competition between the great castrati and various instruments, of which surprisingly the trumpet was the most popular. Castrati like Farinelli (1705–1782) had amazing international careers rewarded by staggering sums of money

– more like today's film stars than opera singers. Furthermore, they had a wonderful time with the ladies, offering as they did, reassurance in an age of few or no contraceptive techniques. Poor Farinelli had to pay dearly for the admiration he aroused, however. For twenty-five years he found himself more or less trapped in the Spanish Court, forced to sing the same arias every night for months at a time to the moronic Philip V, who would then attempt to imitate him with dismal howlings. (Domenico Scarlatti had had to endure much the same thing a few years before – hence we have over 600 magnificent sonatas.) Charles III in Naples was another eighteenth-century monarch who enjoyed throwing his weight around. He would pelt his courtiers with cream buns from the royal box – they just had to grin and bear it. Only in the still-surviving habit of dressing up to go to the opera does some of the feeling of royal influence remain. I met an old lady in Canareggio in Venice who said that she loved opera and listened to it on the radio, but had never been to La Fenice opera house. 'Why not?' I asked. '*Ma signore, non ho i vestiti.*' (But sir, I haven't the clothes.) I tried to explain that these days you don't exactly have to have a tiara to get in. She shook her head sadly '*Ormai è troppo tardi*' (And now it is too late).

RIGOLETTO

*Giuseppe Verdi, Sadler's Wells Theatre,
London, 1950*

Bees can be dangerous, dogs and horses disastrous, but I am most grateful to Mrs C. A. Rogers for pointing out that *cats* can be just as bad. Rigoletto was about to throw into the river the sack containing, not, as he believes, the dead body of his enemy, but of his beloved daughter Gilda. As the singer approached the tragic climax the audience started laughing. He turned round to find that a kitten had wandered on to the stage and was clawing at the sack containing the 'dead' body – which was giving surreptitious jerks as the claws sank in. The singer finally found a moment in which to boot the animal from the stage.

The AUDIENCE

Some opera disasters are caused by the audience. This seems hard to believe in Anglo-Saxon countries, where the audience tends to be an essentially passive, timid body, watching the goings-on on stage with a blissfully willing suspension of disbelief. Not so in Italy, however, even today – performances often take on the character of a dialogue between audience and performers. '*Dormi, maestro*,' they cry when the music goes too slowly; '*Vai a casa!*' (Go home), I heard the Romans shout at an unfortunate tenor in *Pagliacci*, his crime being mere physical inability to repeat '*Vesti la giubba*' for a *fourth* time – poor man, he really was Pagliaccio by then – '*la gente paga è rider vuole qua . . .*' In Parma tenors are regularly hounded to the station by dissatisfied connoisseurs, the fee they have paid to the local 'claque' humiliatingly returned to its leader, who then leads the booing . . .

A charming audience interjection comes from . . .

DON CARLO
Giuseppe Verdi, La Scala, Milan, 1970

A very fine performance with Placido Domingo, Nicolai Ghiaurov, Martti Talvela, Shirley Verrett and Rita Orlandi Malaspina. As Claudio Abbado began the opening of King Philip's aria – an incomparable portrayal by Ghiaurov – a voice from the gods cried '*Io trovo questa musica molto lenta e noiosa*' ('I find this music remarkably slow and boring') – this *à propos* that divine cello theme, never better played. Incredible! The comment was addressed not to us, nor even to Claudio Abbado or the orchestra, but to Giuseppe Verdi, dead for over sixty years.

Certainly the audience can be insulting and annoying, but can it become physically dangerous? Yes indeed! Not for nothing did the Austrians wait for Verdi performances in Venice with fear and trepidation – in those cries of '*Viva VERDI*' was hidden the King's name – Vittorio Emanuele, Re d'Italia; every time *Nabucco* was given the theatre had to be surrounded with troops because of the audience reaction to '*Va pensiero*', that moving plaint of an enslaved people. Even in the twentieth century *Don Carlo* is still dynamite in Spain – banned from the Madrid stage throughout the Franco regime. What happens, though, if the audience identifies not merely with the general situation but with the characters themselves? For this we really have to go to Sicily . . .

OTELLO
Giuseppe Verdi, Catania, 1963

The baritone Giancarlo Lombardi, was somewhat puzzled to find himself booed off stage as Iago even before he had sung the *Credo*! He made discreet enquiries, to find to his amazement that the problem lay not at all in his singing, but in the fact that his mere appearance as Iago reminded the audience too much of the traditional villain 'Gano' in the Sicilian puppet show – Gano is the wretch who betrays the Christian knights to the Infidels. Sure enough, returning to his dressing room the following night, he was terrified to find himself threatened by a man standing in the passage, knife in hand, hissing the word, 'Judas'. It seems Lombardi was actually lucky – according to Claudio of the Bellini Bar, Palermo, a previous exponent of the part had to dodge a hail of bullets from an infuriated marksman well positioned in the Prima Galleria.

One might well examine any possible overlap between operatic and other kinds of disasters, for example natural or political disasters. Surely this field might yield some inexplicable coincidences, some of those Jungian simultaneities ... On the political front, how strange it is that opera should be thought in the Western world to have this blandly élitist character, when revolution and subversion of every kind form its entire theme – was it *really* necessary for Verdi to change *Un Ballo in Maschera* from Stockholm to seventeenth-century Boston? We must remember though that the Communist world adopts the opposite approach, usually in highly exaggerated form. A splendid Handel Festival in East Berlin in 1960 described the courtly Handel as 'the people's composer – a true revolutionary' while no one who saw it could ever forget the Zagreb Opera's 1970 production of *The Magic Flute* in modern dress with the Queen of the Night as a feather-boa-ed Chicago moll in a white Rolls Royce accompanied by black gangsters ... (on second thoughts these were of course corrupt Capitalist blacks as opposed to Sarastro's good Communist negroes).

In Italy, intrusions from the political world have almost but not quite caused a fiasco on many twentieth-century occasions. At the première of *Tosca* in 1900, for instance, the conductor Leopoldo Mugnone was shaking like a leaf because of a bomb threat to Queen Margherita who was present – he had good reason, since a bomb had been thrown backstage during a Toscanini *Otello* shortly before (it failed to explode) and the King – Umberto I – was in fact assassinated a few months later. Fascist violence erupted into La Scala in 1923 when Toscanini defied a group of Blackshirts who instructed him to play 'Giovinezza' before curtain-up – and again at the 1926 première of *Turandot*, unfortunately scheduled for the Fascist Empire Day – Toscanini won again with his 'Choose! It's Mussolini or me!' Today, the opening of La Scala each December serves rather as a focus for leftist discontent; disaffected students, workers and others pelt the diamond-encrusted bourgeoises as they step from their limousines with '*cachi*' (persimmons) – squashy fruit about the size of an avocado pear which burst on impact into an enormous sticky yellow-red morass. This ritual act is accompanied by suitable slogans, such as '*Valpreda vi augura buon divertimento*' ('Valpreda wishes you a good time' – he is one of the left's imprisoned 'martyrs'). Next day the winter round of strikes and pay claims can begin, and Milan grits its teeth for another '*caldo inverno*' (hot winter).

OTELLO
Opera/South, New Orleans, 1955

And so to the deep South. Opera/South is an admirable institution – possibly the only all-black opera company in the world and the starting point of many of the great coloured singers now before the public. On this occasion the company embarked on *Otello*, but the illness of both the tenor and, at the last moment, his under-study obliged them to look outside the company for the lead singer. Since the only substitute available was white, the performance constituted the first known production of an all-black *Otello* with Otello as the only white man. Brilliant – of course Otello becomes in this interpretation a brutal white mercenary hired by a highly sophisticated African state – one cannot help thinking of the dramatic effect, not so much in the opera, where the librettist Boïto plays down Otello's blackness, but rather in the play, where we have but to reverse a line or two – 'Thy soul is as white as thy face . . .'

WAGNERIAN EVENTS

One might have thought that the Wagner operas would yield a rich crop of unfortunate happenings, though the worst I have seen was merely a Brünnhilde at the Fenice Theatre in Venice encountering sudden visibility problems by putting on her helmet the wrong way round. In fact the old master of stagecraft seems to have made his operas very nearly disaster-proof – that is, of course, once you accept the conventions imposed by the work and whatever style of production is on offer, and of course assuming that all concerned have the sheer stamina for the task. Bernard Levin claims to have seen a *Siegfried* involving three different Siegfrieds, one for each act; the most I can offer is two Walther von Stolzings changing over between Acts II and III of *Meistersinger* (quite satisfactory if you discount the fact that one was singing in German and the other in Serbo-Croat). Very long intervals before the last third of the *Meistersinger* do, it is true, always suggest that Walther has lost his voice, which in turn inspires the delightful thought that Pogner really ought to give his daughter to the only other contestant – Beckmesser – by walkover. Not that he hasn't already won her on merit – I entirely subscribe to the admirable view of Erik Smith (of Philips) that Beckmesser's song is anyway incomparably better (especially as regards the words) than Walther's maundering rubbish. May we not hope for a modern production which will at last give us a decent ending, like the old Covent Garden Ring cycles which used to end with *Siegfried*? Some sort of justice for Beckmesser is surely not beyond the capacity of modern Wagner production; and indeed now that Patrice Chérau has shown us that a dinner-jacketed Wotan is acceptable, one feels that a mere

'disaster' would hardly be noticed. Perhaps the return to a 'new realism' will give us once again the chance to see at Bayreuth the (stuffed) swan shot by Parsifal fall on the head of an extra, laying him out cold. Meanwhile, here is a little gem from New York.

LOHENGRIN
Richard Wagner, Metropolitan Opera, 1936

As Lauritz Melchior – perhaps the greatest of Lohengrins – ended '*O König hör*' in the last act, the swan-boat arrived – amid that exquisite orchestral radiance – exactly on time, but alas took off again before the tenor had a chance to get into it. Trapped in what can only be called a totally untenable position, Melchior looked up at the audience and asked in the exhausted, resigned tone of one who has, say, missed the number 47 night bus '*Wenn geht der nächste Schwann?*' – When does the next swan go? Apparently, he was quoting Leo Slezak, stuck thirty years before in the same position.

Perhaps apocryphally, a tenor singing the role at Covent Garden in the 1950s is said to have impaled himself particularly painfully on the swan's tail and shouted out 'Webster must go!'

SIEGFRIED

Royal Opera House, Covent Garden,
London, 1937

I can't think of an opera act which rises to a single climactic moment in quite the same way as *Siegfried* Act I. One is somehow simultaneously excited on a primitive level by those barbaric cries of '*Nothung, Nothung*' and also caught up in sympathy with any tenor singing that diabolical part. (Bravo, Alberto Remedios at the English National Opera, surely emerging as the Siegfried of our generation.) As the sword is slowly forged before our eyes – symbol of the strength which will destroy Wotan's spear – we begin to wait in agonies of impatience for him to cleave the anvil on '*So schneidet Siegfrieds Schwert*'. In 1937 it was again Lauritz Melchior who squared himself to the task when – horror of horrors – the anvil fell apart three seconds before he hit it. At least that's the first occasion I know of when this occurred – according to Lionel Salter it became so regular an event that younger members of the Covent Garden audience thought it was part of the story, in the same way as they assumed that Wagner dragons would quite normally come on stage with one eye inter-mittently flashing and the other out. Perhaps they felt that the dragon was somehow a reflection of Wotan, with his one eye – abstruse symbolism rather than faulty wiring.

DAS RHEINGOLD
English National Opera, London, 1976

The first scene of the opera is set at the bottom of the Rhine, and the stage instructions call for the three Rhinemaidens to 'swim' around the stage. For this production, the whole of the stage was bathed in aqueous light and the three singers were attached to constantly rising and falling wires. It was both pretty and effective (though it must have been murder to sing in such conditions) until, one evening, very, very slowly and inexorably the safety curtain descended, at first hiding the Rhinemaidens only on their upward journeys, so that the sound of their voices was alternately muffled and *fortissimo*, and then concealing everything except occasional glimpses of their descending feet. With enormous aplomb they sang on, and it was the orchestra whose nerve failed. As the safety curtain hit the stage the music finally died away in a ragged shower of wrong notes. The management's explanation was that a leak had developed in the hydraulic system . . .

For the following I am again indebted to Bernard Levin . . .

DIE WALKÜRE
Royal Opera House, Covent Garden,
London, 1961

This is Hans Hotter's great fall from the mountain-top at the end of *Die Walküre*. The producer had decided to start the magic fire by having flashbulbs explode as Wotan struck the rock with his spear, with the consequence that everybody in the house was temporarily blinded. This hardly mattered for Brünnhilde, who had after all just been put to sleep, but it caused Hotter, turning to leave the stage, to miss his footing and fall from the mountain with a crash (he was covered in stage armour) 'like a bomb hitting a corrugated-iron factory'. Presumably fearing that somebody who did not know the opera might conclude that it ends with Wotan being so struck with remorse that he commits suicide by hurling himself into the valley, Hotter gallantly climbed back into position, thus giving the audience, which had already had its money's worth and a bit over, the extra pleasure of seeing the singer's head suddenly appear from the chasm into which it had vanished, to be followed by the rest of him.

DIE WALKÜRE
*Royal Opera House, Covent Garden,
London, 1956*

Hans Hotter still remembers this slightly less alarming incident. He was for some reason delayed in putting on a new, enormous cloak before his entry in Act III – 'Wo ist Brünnhild?' Grabbing it from the dressing room he cast it round his shoulders and strode on to the stage, to confront an inexplicably mirthful audience. The fact was that towering above his shoulders, invisible to him, was the coat-hanger on which the cloak had been hanging. It was a fluffy, *pink* coat-hanger. He sailed through the act, his mighty stage-presence doubtless soon convincing the audience that Wotan without a coat-hanger is no Wotan at all. As Ernest Newman said, he is surely 'the only man in the world who can actually step on stage and persuade you that he is God.'

Joan Sutherland is also not an artist to be put off by minor problems of costume . . .

BEATRICE DI TENDA
Vincenzo Bellini, Teatro San Carlo, Naples, 1961

During a performance of the last act of Luchino Visconti's magnificent staging of this unjustly neglected Bellini opera, Dame Joan's petticoat sank ever

lower – and irreversibly, since Beatrice is on stage all the time. However, it was not until the final curtain call that it hit the deck completely – to be plucked from around her feet by the tenor Renato Cioni. He waved it in the air with Latin gallantry, to the audience's cries of *'Viva, viva la Stupenda!'*

SIEGFRIED
Manchester, 1976

Siegfried approaches with the usual trepidation the sleeping form of Brünnhilde, dreading that moment of potential comedy when he removes her breastplate and starts back with the words, *'Das ist kein Mann.'* His heroic bearing eliminated any possibility of audience titters at this point, but even his professionalism was strained to the limit when he saw beneath the breastplate a note – DO NOT DISTURB, EARLY MORNING TEA 7.30 A.M.'

IDOMENEO
W. A. Mozart, La Fenice, Venice, 1981

I don't want to knock La Fenice – if there is a more beautiful theatre in the world I'd like to know of it – but it appears to be ill-fated when it comes to any form of experimental production. (I did once see there the worst production of a Shakespeare play which I have ever seen.

It was *The Winter's Tale*, and it so happened that Ezra Pound was among the audience. Next day, I met him at a lunch party given in his honour and we asked him what he had thought of it. In his usual laconic way he looked up and said 'Ham and Bear', which I thought summed it up perfectly.) On this occasion we had an *Idomeneo*, again decorated in black plastic, but with an attempt being made to represent the sea. A posse of dancers had been recruited to represent mermaids, seals and what appeared to be whales, also a number of boy dancers were lying around apparently pretending to be waves. All these people were in some way linked together, suggesting that it would be exceedingly alarming (my informant tells me) if, as was perfectly possible, someone suddenly needed to leave the stage in a hurry for some pressing personal reason. A kind of conga of waves, mermaids, seals – and whales – would have to leave the stage and return.

DIE WALKÜRE
La Scala, 1959

In one of innumerable disasters depending on the fact that one of the principals is taller than the other, Siegmund (Wolfgang Windgassen), who was wearing built-up shoes, lost his balance after pulling out Nothung from the tree trunk, and on the run-up to Sieglinde fell over backwards on the raked stage. Seeing him approaching at a tremendous speed, she simply opened her legs and he sailed through beneath, ending up near the orchestra pit, ten yards down stage. It must have been one of the great slides in Wagner – he was later described as a polar bear coming down a water chute – as opposed to mere falls such as Hans Hotter's in Covent Garden in 1948, which caused Philip Hope-Wallace to wonder publicly, 'Need the stage be built up like the Mappin Terraces at the Zoo? Valkyries are not antelopes . . .'

LOHENGRIN
New York, The Metropolitan Opera, 1937

This is yet another magnificent Melchior story. He was all set for the moment in Act III when the evil Telramund tricks him in the bridal chamber. Imagine his utter consternation when, on diving under the bed to seize his hidden sword he found that the incompetent stage management had forgotten to put it there. Bereft of weapons he therefore met the astonished Telramund with a short left to the jaw – it did the trick.

LOHENGRIN
The Paris Opéra

Again in Act III, the tenor singing Lohengrin ran into trouble, but this time not because he had lost his sword, but because like our Irish tenor on p. 87 he was unfortunately suffering from malaria. Perhaps his identification with the part had therefore become too complete – he simply found that his Elsa was so ravishingly attractive that the third time she was foolish enough to break his commandment by asking him his name he mentally jumped straight to the end of the opera and replied in the most ringing tones, *'Dein ritter, ich bin Lohengrin bekannt'* (I, your knight, am called Lohengrin). Fortunately the swan operators were not expecting this cue or we might have had the shortest *Lohengrin* ever . . .

Here it would appear that the *souffleur* (prompter) was taken by surprise. How could he imagine that Lohengrin would forget the most important moment in his entire role? On the other hand, it is the duty of the *souffleur* to assume the worst. In Italy his task is made yet more demanding by the fact that he is also expected to conduct. It is not commonly realized that the conductor in the orchestra pit is not normally visible to the singers, nor, due to the enormous noise they are making themselves, is the orchestra audible. Hence the proliferation of closed-circuit television sets in modern opera houses and the vast artistic importance of the *souffleur* in older ones. The problem however is that the *souffleur* may actively disagree with the conductor's tempi to the point of deliberately establishing a completely different speed for the singers to that which prevails in the orchestra pit. An example . . .

CARMEN
Georges Bizet, Palermo, 1981

The leader of the orchestra, Gottfried Schmidt of Cologne (affectionately known in Germany as Fritz the Violin), told me of the orchestra's success in beating the singers to the end of the second act quintet by a full five seconds. The sound suggested Bizet as reinterpreted by a rather wild disciple of Webern. Nor did Gottfried think that matters were likely to improve. 'Next time we shall beat them by ten seconds,' he said proudly. Unfortunately I didn't stay in Palermo long enough to find out if he was right . . .

There certainly is a special art to producing *Tristan*. During the second act it is obviously essential that the two lovers be lying down. It is, however, very difficult for them, if they are lying anywhere realistically near each other, to see the conductor. If, however, they are not lying near each other, the impact of the duet is, shall we say, somewhat diminished. My brother, D. V. H. Vickers, tells me that the first time he saw *Tristan* was in Germany and that they were *not* lying near each other. The lady singing Isolde appeared to be lying on a mattress; it was only when she got up that he realized, as he put it, that she *was* the mattress.

TRISTAN UND ISOLDE
Richard Wagner, La Fenice, Venice, 1981

Venice is of course always associated with disaster of one form or another, but this particular *Tristan* seems to have attracted the worst that La Serenissima can offer. The set appeared to be made entirely of black plastic, but the remarkable point of interest in the production occurred when Isolde says 'Put out the fateful light', in the second act. By some electronic mistake, every light in the theatre and auditorium chose this precise moment to blaze out. Peter Maag, conducting, carried on with his usual professionalism despite gales of laughter from the audience.

ACTS of GOD

As we have seen, disasters are so much the stuff of opera that there seems hardly room for *real* natural disasters to obtrude on to the scene. *Al fresco* opera of course presents problems – it was alarming to see the mistral suddenly getting up during an open-air *Walküre* at the 1976 Orange Festival in the south of France and blowing all the orchestral parts away at the same moment, or the floating stage at Bregenz drifting off into the middle of the lake, complete with orchestra. Within the opera house fire is in reality the true danger, though the only major disaster of this sort for some years seems to have been the destruction of the Cairo Opera House in 1970 (with the loss of the sets and costumes for the original *Aida*) – a somewhat ironic mishap in view of the fact that the main Cairo fire station was in fact situated in part of the opera house itself.

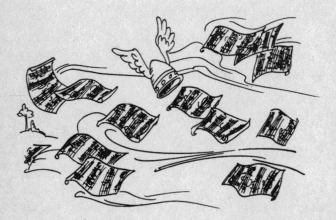

Flood is less common, though sets involving real water have their dangers, of course . . .

TURANDOT
Giacomo Puccini, Rome Opera, 1954

In the last scene the set showed one of those meandering oriental streams with Turandot standing on one bank and the tenor, Carlo Gasparini, standing on the other, with a little Chinese–Milanese rustic bridge between them. Gasparini's instructions were simple – when she cries 'Mio nome è Amor!' he was to turn, charge across the bridge and grasp Turandot in his arms. In fact, he turned, charged, forgot the bridge, tried to leap the stream, tripped and fell in, thus very nearly joining the disconsolate ranks of Turandot's former admirers . . .

A real earthquake might make a very effective interjection in a great many operas, but I know of only one case . . .

CAVALLERIA RUSTICANA
Pietro Mascagni, San Francisco, 1938

With Lily Pons, no less. She made her entry as Santuzza in a 'Sicilian' donkey cart – *you* know, ethnic painting all over it, and the donkey wearing a straw hat with holes for its ears. Suddenly there came that unnerving quivering which every inhabitant of San

Francisco experiences from time to time. It was too much for the donkey. With a great shrieking *eeeaw* he leapt in the air and charged across the stage, throwing Lily Pons out of the back of the cart and bringing down all the scenery.

TESS
Frédéric d'Erlanger, Naples, 1906

But perhaps the most dramatic of nature's inter-ventions occurred during the first night of Frédéric d'Erlanger's opera based on Thomas Hardy's *Tess of the d'Urbervilles*. According to the Hardy scholar Dr Desmond Hawkins, d'Erlanger wrote to Hardy from Milan in April 1906, complaining that 'Mount Vesuvius behaved most unkindly to me' and that his weeks of patient rehearsal in Naples had been rewarded during the first act by a violent eruption. The audience was in any case small – as the popu-lation had feared an eruption for some days – and their 'state ... it is hardly necessary for me to describe'. The theatre was closed down next day by the municipality, despite a 'hearty reception' and favourable press coverage for that part of the opera which the terrified company had managed to present. When Hardy heard of this debacle, he remarked, characteristically, that it was only to be expected, as being all of a piece with Tess's career.

Vesuvius seems, indeed, to have a certain antipathy towards the intrusion into Naples of English opera plots – and hero-ines, for that matter. It had already erupted before during the San Carlo debut of Mrs Billington, the first great English soprano of the early nineteenth century. She was howled off the stage by an infuriated audience who consid-ered that the mountain was rightly protesting against the appearance at the San Carlo of a 'Protestant heretic'.

(Fortunately she was able to find some consolation in the simultaneous loss of her unwanted husband, a double-bass virtuoso she had married at sixteen.) Actually, the attitude of Neapolitans towards their opera house is very emotional. I was talking to one during an interval at La Scala who insisted that the essence of the San Carlo is that it is '*maschio*' (masculine). 'What about the Fenice in Venice?' I hazarded. '*Ah, quella è femmina.*' 'And this one here?' (looking around at the glorious Scala). A sneer. '*Questo qui, caro signore, Questo è neutro.*'

'HAIR-BREADTH
SCAPES'

This chapter begins by recalling some of the innumerable occasions when disaster has been averted by inspired improvization and a masterly understanding of the exigencies of the moment. Somehow, the march of events in opera prevents memory loss, for instance, from being quite so dangerous as in the straight theatre – one can't quite imagine in an opera house the famous story about Gielgud and Richardson who, after listening to a prompt three times in complete silence, turned to the prompter with the words 'We know the line, man, we just can't remember which of us says it.' On the other hand, the act of singing as you plunge on to the stage is so nerve-racking that an entry at the wrong moment is quite a hazard, as is a sudden, immediate freeze – I remember idiotically remarking to a soprano in the wings 'I bet you can't even remember which opera this is' – sure enough she stepped on stage and couldn't. Even Tito Gobbi's début at La Scala, as a Herald in Pizzetti's *Orseolo* (conducted by the composer), consisted in bawling out the words '*La Signoria del Doge e del Senato*' half a minute too soon, in the middle of Tancredi Pasero's most important aria. '*Cretino, chi t'ha mandato qui?*' (Idiot, who sent you here?) were therefore the words addressed to Gobbi from the Scala rostrum . . .

Here, however, is something for connoisseurs of *averted* disaster . . .

THE MAGIC FLUTE
Glyndebourne Festival, 1964

In Franco Enriquez and Emmanuele Luzzati's enchanting production, the scenery consisted of a number of free-standing triangular pillars, on each face of which a different coloured pattern was painted. Thus, for the scene to change from, say, the forest to Sarastro's temple, the stagehand inside each pillar merely turned round through 120 degrees. Near the beginning of the second half of the opera, during a snatch of dialogue between Heinz Blankenburg as Papageno and Ragnar Ulfung as Tamino, two unfortunate stagehands lost their balance and crashed, complete with pillars, to the ground, letting out involuntary and clearly audible cries for help as they did so. Blankenburg looked at Ulfung. Ulfung looked at Blankenburg, and together they walked backstage and with much ad-libbing in German – including a free advertisement for the strength-giving powers of Guinness – heaved the pillars upright again. Rubbing their hands with satisfaction they then returned to the front of the stage to continue the opera – but not before the Glyndebourne audience, as always in a jovial mood after the dinner interval, had burst into a tremendous round of applause.

Nor are singers a whit less resourceful, as anyone who works with them knows. At a production of my own of Philidor's *Blaise le Savetier* at the French Institute, London, 1976, a quarter-inch steel pin was supposed to hold in place the false front of the *armoire* in which the philandering land-lord, Monsieur Pince, is hiding. Watching in the wings, I was appalled to see the pin break and the *armoire* door begin slowly to open (thus destroying the entire plot) when, with an ease which positively enhanced the dramatic situation, the tenor Emile Belcourt as the outraged husband casually leant against it for the exact amount of time required for Garrick Jones within to get a grip on it – the audience of course noticing nothing in the excitement of the near-confrontation between husband and lover. Belcourt as Loge is of course also – like most Loges – a doughty hand at rebuilding the pile of gold which the stupid gods have knocked down (or rather, the designer and producer have made incapable of standing up) with a scornful and supercilious expression exactly fitting the character. A yet more charming example of stage improvisation, however, is this from *The Quiet Showman*, Montague Haltrecht's life of Sir David Webster . . .

DIE WALKÜRE
Covent Garden Manchester, 1956

The performance was a splendid one, conducted by Reginald Goodall and with the famous Hilde Konetzni as Sieglinde. He [Sir David] loved describing the moment of great ecstasy in the love duet when quite suddenly she performed a beautiful sweeping movement, one he'd not seen before, and ended kneeling at her lover's feet. He was deeply moved, and tears sprang to his eyes. He would go on to explain that what had actually happened was that the lady had *lost a tooth* and had seen it caught in the light – gleaming like Rhinegold! Her swooping joy was the joy of discovery, not the ecstasy of love. There was panic in the interval, with Konetzni not at all sure she could continue with a tooth missing. Stage director Elizabeth Latham happily had an inspiration. Wouldn't chewing gum keep it in? She sent out for some. It worked. It *just* kept the tooth steady for the rest of the performance.

SIEGFRIED
Royal Opera House, Covent Garden, 1955

However, even worse than a Sieglinde losing her tooth is surely a Siegfried who loses his sword. At Covent Garden the property master seemed to have grasped the idea that Siegfried has to forge a complete sword from various pieces, but not the fact that he must finally be able to show the audience the finished article and even split an anvil with it. Alas it was not until halfway through the forging scene that Wolfgang Windgassen realized that only the fragments had been supplied, and he was therefore faced with the urgent necessity of actually forging Nothung in good earnest, for the first time in the history of the *Ring*, and on an anvil made of cardboard. Responding calmly to the challenge, he allowed his run-up to the anvil to take him further and further towards the wings, where he managed to collect the complete sword and bring it on under his cloak undetected by the audience.

DON GIOVANNI
City Center, New York, 1960

A terrified new Don Ottavio mentally reversed the order of his arias, walked on stage and began '*Il mio tesoro*' instead of '*Dalla sua pace*'. It is said that the orchestra, under Julius Rudel, had such mastery of the score that as one man they instantaneously cut to the correct bar a hundred odd pages later, with such aplomb that the audience assumed that for some reason the arias had been deliberately reversed.

A notable example of cool teamwork between Tito Gobbi and an unknown member of the Covent Garden chorus is recounted in the great singer's autobiography *My Life*.

UN BALLO IN MASCHERA
Royal Opera House, Covent Garden, 1954

Gobbi was rushed in at an afternoon's notice to replace an indisposed Anckerstroem, only to find that the production was in the original version – eighteenth-century Sweden instead of seventeenth-century Boston. Gobbi had not been informed of this and had never sung in the Swedish version. His experience therefore, though doubtless extremely puzzling, did not become positively alarming until the last act, when he suddenly realized that he lacked a knife to assassinate Gustavus III – otherwise the Earl of Warwick – indeed, that his position was that of our soldiers in *Tosca* but in reverse – he knew whom to execute but not how. The chorus member managed to read his mind and, incredibly, to obtain a pistol (presumably from one of the guards). 'What do I need a pistol for?' mutters Gobbi, still all set for the stabbing. 'You *shoot* him, now!' And Anckerstroem gave his rival the *coup de grâce* with the correct weapon.

Hamburg

Finally, Peter Ustinov found himself directing an opera in what is without doubt *the* most technically advanced opera stage in the world – the Hamburg Opera House. There, whole sets wait in an enormous structure beside the wings and slide into place at the touch of a button. The technicians are quite incredibly efficient, and yet – there was one man who was totally hopeless. With him, everything went wrong. He dropped a hammer from the flies, narrowly missing the stage director's head. Whole sets fell down as he approached. The computerized lighting track went bananas and darkness fell over all . . . Eventually Mr Ustinov asked him to explain exactly who he was and why they kept him on. 'Ah, you see, they keep me here to *humanize* them.' An admirable reply, but surely there must be more to it than that. Ustinov went on to ask, 'But *why* do you in fact make all these incredible mistakes?' 'Ah, you see, it's a long family tradition.' 'What? You mean there are *more* of you, a whole *family*?' 'Oh yes, – you should have seen my father.' 'What did he do?' 'Well, he was stage director of the Klagenfurt Opera and he made the most incredible mistakes, much worse than anything of mine . . . But – one day he achieved the impossible – he got it *all* right. The opera was *William Tell*, very much the thing for Klagenfurt of course, and watching from the stage manager's place in the wings, he could *see* that it was perfect – all the sets in place, the chorus in position, the animals behaving, the prompter prompting, the singers singing and the orchestra (audibly) playing.' 'So what went wrong?' 'Oh just one little thing – *the curtain never went up . . .*'

And in those days it could have been possible. Just.

GENERAL MAYHEM

Thank you Mrs Jenny Hill for this transcendental story – raising Australia at a stroke to the level of London, San Francisco, nay, even New York, as a forum for great operatic disasters.

SALOMÉ
Richard Strauss, date unknown

A somewhat staid Australian city hardly seems a likely choice for a production of *Salomé*, but the young iconoclastic producer was determined to give the townspeople the shock of their lives with this rich orgy of German incest, necrophilia and doom. He instructed the property department to make an exceptionally gory and revolting head of John the Baptist to be brought on at the end of the great final scene where Salome insists on kissing his mouth. As rehearsals wore on, however, the usual rift on the matter of good taste developed between the producer and the director of the theatre board. After endless arguments the producer was persuaded to the point of allowing the head to be brought in covered with a white cloth. However, by this time the soprano, an imported East German lady of 'commanding and awesome stature', had fallen out with the stagehands, with the result that when the first night came, the audience stayed transfixed until the final scene, all concerned looking on with agonized apprehension as the silver platter bearing the Baptist's head was slowly carried on. 'Daughter of Herodias, you blaspheme,' cried Herod. 'I care not, I will kiss his mouth,' Salome replied. The head got nearer, the orchestra lashed itself up yet again into a necrophiliac, erotic frenzy, the moment came, she snatched away the cloth . . . and on the charger was a pile of ham sandwiches.

She collapsed in a heap of laughter and the curtain was rung down.

From Australia, we move to South America, where opera is of course largely indistinguishable from real life. Anyway, it is surprisingly well entrenched, even though the national languages are Spanish and Portuguese. I was amazed to find a lively tradition of slightly chaotic opera in Rio de Janeiro; unusual hazards abound – it was on one occasion, for example, quite impossible to hear Carlo Bergonzi's 'O dolci baci' because an enormous samba band had struck up for the carnival rehearsals in the square outside.

The opera played a vital role in the 1964 Brazilian Revolution – a typically Brazilian event in every way. The President, Django Goulart, happened to be away on a fact-finding trip to Red China (he was always disappearing without warning – he was once found after three weeks attending a performance of Un Ballo in Maschera in the Pergola Theatre, Florence). On this occasion Brazil's inflation rate had reached two thousand per cent a week in his absence. The army moved – but unfortunately, being Brazil, there were two rival armies; one the rather cultivated Third Army from São Paulo, the other, the distinctly grim Fourth Army from Belo Horizonte. Both had orders to occupy the Presidential Palace in Rio, but found it almost impossible, as does everyone, to get their tanks through the Rio evening rush-hour traffic. They arrived at the Palace simultaneously and after a somewhat tense moment the officers of the two sides conferred; it turned out that the two senior officers of the rival armies were opera fanatics – one a brother of Brazil's leading baritone, Nelson Portela. Portela was singing in La Bohème that night and the officers agreed they had to hear him, coup or no coup: in fact their drive to Rio was an admirable excuse. It is alleged that they rushed off to the Opera House in their armoured personnel-carriers, needless to say leaving their men to play a football match, using the tanks as goal posts. Goulart came charging back from China the next day, but that was probably because he was hoping to hear the opera as well.

Down to the Teatro Colón, proud boast of the Argentine – the largest opera house in the world, or so they say – or is it the New York Met., or La Scala, or the Teatro Massimo, Palermo? Who knows? Anyway a very high standard prevails there both in opera and operatic disasters; several choice examples have occurred. As at Covent Garden, Siegfried's sword either fails to smash the anvil, or the anvil, if controlled from the wings, opens too soon, or if being worked by Siegfried, five or six seconds too late. This, however, is my favourite disaster . . .

DIE WALKÜRE
Richard Wagner, Buenos Aires

Here the stage fire did not have the explosive, blinding effect of the Covent Garden variety, on the other hand it was a little more real when Giampiero Mastromei struck the rock – a great wall of fire appeared, and he was forced to give a remarkable new ironic inflection to the words, '*Nur wer meines Spitzes fürchtet, durchschreite fas Feue nie . . .*' by fleeing from the stage with his beard in flames (an awful fate much dreaded by Scarpias when some silly Tosca puts a candle too near their wigs – apparently this once happened to the young Norman Bailey in Germany, in the late 1960s).

TOSCA
Teatro Colón, Buenos Aires, c. 1950

More *Tosca* horrors – Maria Jeritza tripped up and fell flat on her face in front of Scarpia. No time to get up, so she nobly sang the whole of 'Vissi *d'arte*' lying on her stomach. Quite possible – it is often done lying down, but usually on a chaise longue, lying or bending backwards over Scarpia's table, or some other inconvenient position. The trouble was that the Colón stage is vast and there simply was not any light at the place she was lying – by the time the wandering follow-spots had got her in their searchlight beam she had finished.

From South America, where to go but Ireland? But of course producing opera in Ireland, other than at the delicious Wexford Festival, is fraught with absurd problems and even Wexford, as we shall see, can contribute its disaster. I remember Anthony Besch telling me about working with the Dublin Grand Opera Society years ago: he said that one would arrive having been given, say, forty-eight hours' rehearsal time, to prepare five or six operas; the singers straggling in from various remote areas; absolutely no stage-hands available. Apparently those in command, if asked where a given person was, would invariably give that enchanting/infuriating Irish reply, 'Och, he went to the West.' The result was that the entire stage crew used to be made up of Anthony's grand Irish friends – one would find Jonathan and Desmond Guinness humping enormous pieces of scenery, the Earl of Rosse perched in the flies scattering the artificial snow in *La Bohème* . . . However, the other peril was of course the audience: it was not lacking – it was passionate, enthusiastic, almost Italian in the frequency of its interjections, for instance 'What the devil's all this about then?' at the moment of Leporello's escape in *Don Giovanni*, Act II.

However, this I particularly like . . .

LA BOHÈME
Giacomo Puccini, Dublin Grand Opera Society

The tenor was not merely drunk, but absolutely paralytic. When he was searching on the floor for Mimi's key he bumped into her head so hard that she gave an audible cry of pain. The start of '*Che gelida manina*' was delayed because he literally could not find her hand (admittedly the lighting was not very good). A guffaw went round the house when he finally accepted the invitation to go into the Café Momus – it was obvious that he would be barely able to make it, but he did manage to stagger off on his top C before collapsing in the wings.

The interval was particularly long, with a sweepstake developing among the public as to whether he would reappear or not, and if not, what conceivable excuse would be given; but in fine Irish style the management produced something more unexpected than anyone would have thought possible. The usual sheepish figure in a dinner jacket appeared in front of the curtain and explained that the unfortunate tenor had just returned from a trip to West Africa and was suffering from a slight case of malaria. To which a voice from the gods replied, 'I wish I had a bottle of that, then . . .'

While on the subject of problems arising from the staging of '*Che gelida manina*' we surely ought not to forget Caruso.

LA BOHÈME
New York, The Metropolitan Opera

As is well known, Caruso did not like Nellie Melba – to such a point indeed that, on one occasion, just before he announced her tiny hand was frozen, he grabbed from the wings and placed in it a hot potato. But is this wholly correct? By some accounts it was, even more offensively, a sausage. I trust my readers will devote their considerable scholarship to resolving the precise truth about this incident. For example, Melba's reaction is not recorded: a bottle of champagne for the reader who can devise the most ingenious solution on averted disaster lines. After all, here is this impoverished seamstress in Paris, in the middle of winter; clearly the gift of a hot potato from a complete stranger might be the most exquisite her heart could desire. Should she for instance not clutch it fervently to her lips rather than hitting him in the face with it . . .? Ah well, I leave it to you.

I used to think of French opera audiences as being exclusively on the bourgeois, I-am-there-to-be-seen side. But the dynamic growth of new festivals in France – at Albi for instance – utterly belies this. Research in England shows rather that it is here that the classic audience attitudes die hardest.

DER ROSENKAVALIER
Glyndebourne Festival, 1980

This splendid production was designed by the great Erté, who decided, like Visconti, to backdate the work, in this case into the mid-nineteenth century rather than the world of Art Nouveau. (I myself still cannot see why if *Capriccio* works in an eighteenth-century setting *Rosenkavalier* should not.) Nonetheless Erté's costumes were fabulous: a riot of Second Empire style and colour. This, I think, gives special point to a conversation overheard in the interval:

MAN TO WOMAN: 'Do you know who wrote it?'
WOMAN TO MAN: 'I think it must be Mozart.'
MAN TO WOMAN: 'Why Mozart?'
WOMAN TO MAN: 'Oh you know, because of the costumes.'

OTELLO

Giuseppe Verdi, Royal Opera House,
Covent Garden, 1960s

One of the dottiest of overheard remarks was collected by the publisher of this book at Covent Garden. Mario del Monaco was unable to sing *Otello* and at short notice the hitherto little-known Canadian tenor James McCracken was brought in. It was a debut to match Sutherland's as Lucia a few years before; the entire cast, including Tito Gobbi as Iago, sang like angels and McCracken was, as everyone now knows, a revelation in the title part. As the audience, drained of emotion and exhausted by clapping, left the stalls, one dowager said disapprovingly to another 'My dear, I always knew mixed marriages were a mistake, and that simply *proved* it.'

NORMA

Vincenzo Bellini, Royal Opera House, Covent Garden, 1979

Shirley Verrett revealed that gongs can be as bad as anvils. The gong was a gigantic J. Arthur Rank affair (it had to be, since a stagehands' walk-out had eliminated most of the rest of the set). At the climactic moment in Act II Miss Verrett took the first of her three swipes which would summon the Druids to her side, with such force that the head of the gong stick shot across the stage, where it lay until expertly back-heeled into the wings by a member of the chorus. Poor Miss Verrett, she now had to hit the gong twice more with the bare stick, with the Covent Garden audience in hysterics. At least she did not hit anyone – the nineteenth-century German soprano, Therese Tietjens took such a back swing before striking that she hit the tenor on the nose, laying him out cold. I will add that Bellini had truly bad luck with the use of that gong. How *can* we of the post-Victorian world ever fail to associate it with *Upstairs, Downstairs*? Instead of a priestess calling her people to the sacred fight for liberty, she suggests rather a parlourmaid deputizing for the butler in summoning a tiresomely elderly house party to dinner.

Here is a splendid Covent Garden audience reaction my late friend Philip Hope-Wallace told . . .

LA TRAVIATA
Giuseppe Verdi, Royal Opera House,
Covent Garden, mid-1970s

In the middle of a magnificent performance by Ileana Cotrubas with Alfredo Kraus in the love duet, the curtain was rung down because of a bomb scare. (It was one of those bomb seasons – the conductor, Silvio Varviso, narrowly escaped from a bomb thrown into Scott's restaurant.) Anyway, Philip, who was not to be deterred from opera pleasures by such minor matters, commented afterwards, 'Why didn't John Tooley [the General Administrator] take a more robust view? It was a twenty-minute warning and we were only twelve minutes from the end of the scene.' I fear however that Cotrubas and Kraus would probably have thought that their love, already difficult enough, had become simply too fraught in such circumstances . . .

I should add that nothing on earth has ever been known to scare Mme Cotrubas; her first night as Violetta in *La Traviata* at La Scala was a classic case of averted disaster. It took place before the London incident described above; she was very young and though she knew the role of Violetta, she had never before performed it in public. La Scala were opening the season with a Luchino Visconti *Traviata*, scheduled for a Monday, but both Maria Callas and her understudy fell ill on the preceding Friday; unable to cast from within Italy they telephoned Mme Cotrubas's house near Glyndebourne, but she was shopping in London and her husband was in the bath so he missed the call. When eventually they did get through, he packed their suitcases, put in the *Traviata* score and dashed to London. They arrived at Heathrow just in time for the last plane to Milan, but the airport was fogbound and the flight cancelled. Next morning, Saturday, all flights out of Heathrow were cancelled, and the fog deepened. They stayed at a hotel near the airport. Sunday dawned, Heathrow was clear but Milan-Linate completely fogbound. Monday, the day of the performance, both airports were clear and they arrived in Milan to find a motorcade with police escort headed by the Mayor of Milan, Ghiringelli, the director of La Scala, and a somewhat tense Visconti. They dashed through the specially cleared streets, got through one rehearsal of the more difficult passages of the work; Mme Cotrubas changed into her costume, went on without a moment's rest and received twenty-four curtain calls.

There are, of course, disasters caused by simple absenteeism, frequently due to the proximity to the stage door of a public house, or some other form of hostelry. Berlioz in his *Memoires* points out that it was rare indeed for half the Paris Opera orchestra to be present simultaneously, but the chorus can be even worse. In Italy they have been known to demand extra money for the sort of opera – *The Magic Flute* for instance – which ends with a rousing chorus as opposed to the ideal, *Manon Lescaut*, say, where they can all go home after the third act. Nonetheless . . .

MANON LESCAUT
Giacomo Puccini, The Welsh National Opera,
Brighton Festival, 1978

At the end of a triumphant last act the conductor found that not only the chorus but the entire orchestra had fled, leaving nobody but Manon and Des Grieux on stage. He was in the embarrassing position of profusely thanking a completely empty orchestra pit. Perhaps after a hard stint in Cardiff the legendary attractions of Brighton were just too much, or maybe the Welsh players had heard something about Brighton's opening and closing hours.

LA SONNAMBULA
Vincenzo Bellini, La Scala, Milan, 1963

Bellini's *La Sonnambula* provides surely the hardest possible test of the relationship between singer and orchestra. To somnambulate effectively you have obviously got to have your eyes shut – so no chance of even a modicum of visual help from prompter or conductor. I have always wondered how Callas performed the part with such utter conviction, as at La Scala in 1963.

In 1966 I had the opportunity to ask Luchino Visconti how he had arranged this scene to such great effect. The answer turned out to be that he had made brilliant use of a sense one does not normally associate with the operatic stage – the sense of smell. Visconti invariably wore a handkerchief in his top pocket with a touch of an English fragrance he was fond of. When Callas said she liked it too, it occurred to Visconti to place one of his handkerchiefs on the bed during the sleep-walking scene so that Callas would be guided towards it by the scent alone. This worked perfectly night after night. Only later did it occur to him that it was fortunate indeed that no member of the Scala orchestra – or audience – was wearing that particular scent – otherwise we would have had another, and truly catastrophic opera disaster.

ANNA BOLENA
Gaetano Donizetti, La Scala, Milan, 1961

More homage to Callas. Rarely in operatic history has a singer brought the theatre and real life together with such tremendous effect as when the diva, on her way to execution as Anne Boleyn, looked straight up at the empty box of her enemy the theatre director Ghiringhelli exactly on the words '*Il palco funesto*' (*palco* in Italian happens by a weird coincidence to mean both execution block and opera box).

CARMEN
Los Angeles

Important news from Los Angeles. The reader may recall how, earlier, I described an unfortunate Italian tenor in Mexico City who during an interval in a production of *Carmen* was arrested in a nearby bar by the local police because he looked like Don José – i.e. a military deserter. It now appears that performing *Carmen* can be dangerous even for members of the orchestra. The trumpeter Gilbert Johns of the Los Angeles Philharmonic was standing in the woods surrounding the Hollywood Bowl about to give the off-stage trumpet call which summons Don José back to barracks. A tidy-minded policeman arrested him on the grounds that to be standing in the Robin Hood Dell dressed in a white summer suit holding a trumpet amounted at the least to highly suspicious behaviour. Poor Mr Johns seems to have had more than his fair share of bad luck in open-air events. He was for instance once attacked by a swarm of bees in the middle of Bruckner's second symphony.

DON GIOVANNI
W. A. Mozart

Perhaps all music is really an assault on our emotions, even Mozart. The film of *Don Giovanni* by Joseph Losey is a very good case in point. At the risk of digressing from my already highly digressive theme, what actually does happen in *Don Giovanni*? This seems an excellent place to argue the question of what precisely has occurred at the beginning of the opera. If Giovanni has in fact seduced Donna Anna, her great Act I aria in which she describes the event to Ottavio is a lie. It also appears to stretch the rules of dramatic probability to an absurd extent in that the opera, though called '*dramma giocoso*' by the librettist Da Ponte, is founded in the opera buffa tradition and is therefore basically realistic. On the other hand, everyone feels the erotic content in Donna Anna's words '*Era già alquanto avanzata la notte . . .*' My own feeling is that in eighteenth-century opera, as in all other classical works of art, one should assume that it means what it says unless there is some evident reason to the contrary. If Anna means what she says, we have a much more coherent explanation than if she was in fact seduced by

Giovanni. I think what we are hearing is the lament of a woman who was not seduced by him, but wishes she had been. Surely this is the first rebuff that Don Giovanni has ever received and it initiates the dramatic action and Giovanni's downfall. What Anna is clearly thinking is that her conventional morality (shown in the choice of Ottavio as her fiancé) and her stupid pride caused the death of her father. If this is not so, *why* does she say to Ottavio that she at first mistook Don Giovanni for him? If Ottavio had never visited and made love to Anna at night it would make no sense to say this to him. Clearly she did think it was Ottavio and then found it was an unknown but extremely attractive man. She cried out – just as she says – and Giovanni made good his escape in order to avoid having to fight his way out through a whole pack of the Commendatore's men-at-arms. Otherwise, he would surely have stayed till early morning and then slipped out.

Some allusion must be made to Mr Jeremy Maddon-Simpson's astonishing theory that in the course of the opera Don Giovanni clearly seduces six women. This is rather startling when we compare it with traditional criticisms, such as that of Edward J. Dent (in *Mozart's Operas*) who holds that Giovanni is a complete paper tiger who seduces no one at all. What a classic example of the ambiguity of opera that two such diverse views could be held. Challenged to defend his position, he presented the following Leporello-like list:

1. Donna Anna, at the beginning.
2. Zerlina, in the first act final when she screams off stage (he would have had to have been very quick

IL
COMMENDATORE

about it, but I suppose an expert like Giovanni would just about have had time).

3. Donna Elvira's servant girl, after the serenade, on the assumption that no woman could possibly resist being sung to like that. (I like this theory because there always seems something curious about the immediate switch of emphasis after the serenade away from Don Giovanni on to the escaping Leporello.)

4–5. Two village girls in the interval but before the opening of Act 2. 'If Giovanni was fleeing from the vice squad at the end of Act I, why is he so cheerful when Act II begins?' This point was well taken by Losey in his film – he sets the Act II opening duet with Giovanni disporting himself with a half-naked village girl.

6. Leporello's wife. This I like very much because people in classical opera mean what they say. Not only does Don Giovanni say to Leporello that he ran into a lady who knew him, but when Leporello says 'and suppose it was my wife?' Giovanni roars with laughter and says *'meglio ancora!'*, thus triggering the statue's first pronouncement *'di rider finirai . . .'* and thus the denouement of the opera. Giovanni is blatantly teasing Leporello about an affair he's been having with his wife, probably for some time (it would be absolutely in character and would explain a lot about the curious attachment between Giovanni and Leporello).

As indicated, I only take complete exception to number 1 on this list, partly because I think it would spoil the effect of the work if Elvira and Anna were both women in exactly the same position. They would, in fact, given the conventions of eighteenth-century opera, be deadly rivals. But they are not – they have the utmost sympathy for each other, though their attitudes to Don Giovanni are opposed. Anna wants vengeance, but the feeling is tempered by remorse for the death of her father; Elvira is prepared to the very last moment to love Don Giovanni and to forgive him. For this reason the words in her final recitative, '*aperto veggio il baratro mortal*' was absolutely rightly interpreted by Losey as a religious confession in which she pleads for his soul and her own. Her last words are effectively '*mi tradi quell' Alma ingrata*', while Anna's, be it noted, are addressed to Ottavio '*non mi dir, bell'idol mio, che son io crudel con te.*'

So there we are back where we started. She *does* love Ottavio, and he did come regularly to visit her at night. So there, dear reader, that's my theory – you can disagree with it all you like but I won't budge an inch.

This discussion of *Don Giovanni* and especially Joseph Losey's film of it, reminds us that we must refer to . . .

BORIS GODUNOV
Modest Mussorgski, Paris Opéra, 1980

As with the *Don Giovanni*, most of the conventional opera critics found this one 'delightful, but infuriating'. This was because Losey decided to turn the most basic of all operatic conventions upside down by having the singers in front and the orchestra playing in a sort of gigantic Russian snow hat behind them. Result – the singers sounded as close up as in, say, one of those garish Decca Wagner recordings, while the orchestra sounded as if they were playing in the next room, or possibly even a few streets away. No marks here for Losey, though full marks to that superb baritone Ruggiero Raimondi for an epic Boris.

Having returned to France, we certainly ought to mention what happened at the first known performance in France of one of Sir Thomas Beecham's favourite operas.

LE TABLEAU PARLANT
André Grétry, Lyon, 1936

This is a frothy *opéra bouffe* by the admirable Italian-trained Grétry, who is in fact Belgium's only important composer. (The reader will, I hope recall the Avenue Grétry leading to the Grande Place in Brussels, and, far more important, the superb Restaurant Grétry therein.) The plot is pure *commedia dell'arte* – nasty old Cassandre is in love with his ward Isabelle, who is in love with handsome, young Léandre. Piero and Colombine (Isabelle's confidante) make up the cast of five. About halfway through, Cassandre manages to get into his thick head that there is some kind of hanky-panky going on between all the other characters. He therefore pretends to leave for Paris, but in fact stays skulking round the house, to find out what is going on. Now, the stage is dominated by a giant life-size portrait of Cassandre. At the crucial moment of a love duet between Isabelle and Léandre, Cassandre achieves the ultimate in voyeurism by cutting out the face of the portrait and substituting his own face looking through. (I know this sounds a bit much even for opera but I have seen a production and it is quite hilarious.) So it would have been at Lyon, except that the pre-cut face refused to come out and the singer was so annoyed that when he got behind it he slipped and the whole thing – man, picture, face, the lot – came crashing to the ground. I think the reason was that to get to the face height he had to stand on a table – fatal.

CARMEN
Georges Bizet, Bologna, 1958

In the Lilas Pastia act both Don José and Escamillo fell off two separate tables, in José's case at the end of his flower aria. What a dope – no wonder Carmen turns him down. As a matter of fact, I have always thought that the recruitment of Don José suggests disturbing thoughts about the military standards of the Spanish army – one can hardly imagine him leading an effective *coup* for instance. Similarly, in Escamillo's case one wonders how a man incapable of standing on a table for three minutes without falling over would have much chance in the bullring.

Anyway, with tables the problem is not how you get on the thing, but how on earth you get off it. If you step off it via a chair or bench (*Carmen*, Palermo 1981) it looks hopelessly weak. The only thing is to jump off it but then you must have some goal, aim or objective, preferably someone's arms.

COSÌ FAN TUTTE
W. A. Mozart, Venice, 1974

This beautiful production, originally by Günther Rennert, had some splendid table-jumping in the first scene. Rennert very sensibly sets this in an inn (I cannot think why this is not always done – where else would one find three men making sordid bets) and there are therefore plenty of tables. Fernando jumped on one to deliver *'una bella serenata'* and Guglielmo onto another for *'in onor di Citerea'*. Here they looked perfectly natural with Alfonso on the ground between them. When he said *'saro anche io tra i convitati'* they both jump down simultaneously, and the three men immediately take hands to swear the oath. It was all highly effective.

Writing this here in Florence I am reminded of an event which was not an operatic disaster exactly, but a true operatic tragedy . . .

EGMONT

Goethe/Ludwig van Beethoven, Palazzo Pitti, Florence, 1967

'But it is not an opera' the reader is crying. Well to be precise it is a 'melodrama', but when you hear the whole work with all six pieces of the Beethoven incidental music (not just the famous overture) and when these are played by a large symphony orchestra in front of the stage conducted by Gianandrea Gavazzeni and the epic staging is by Visconti, we surely have more opera than anything else.

As the rehearsals went on, the text and music became even more integrated. During the Beethoven pieces – some of considerable length – the actors would freeze, forming a tableau superbly expressive of the emotional point reached (e.g. as when Egmont hands the Spanish Governor his sword). The dress rehearsal came – open air in the Pitti Palace courtyard on a perfect June evening. The fabulous setting and costumes – the light glinting on the breast-plates of the Spanish guards – suggested now a Rembrandt, now a Velazquez come to life. I had the pleasure of watching this sitting next to Marcello Mastroianni – we were both riveted, hypnotized. Next evening, the opening – half an hour before the start the heavens opened and it rained as only Florence knows how. And believe it or not, it did so with absolute regularity for the scheduled week of the performances. The general public never saw it once and it was never repeated. Poor Visconti – but even the greatest are at the mercy of wind and weather. His film team for *Death In Venice* was kept idle for fifteen days because the cameraman was unhappy about the light for one single shot . . .

CARMEN
Heidelberg

The conductor Ian Reid, recalls, 'When I conducted *Carmen* in Heidelberg, Don José discovered too late that he had forgotten to bring the knife on stage to stab Carmen in the last scene. He decided to strangle her instead. The girl playing Carmen thought he had gone insane and fought back like a tigress. Somehow, she managed to go on singing throughout a prolonged and somewhat muted strangulation.'

ALBERT EINSTEIN

While this is not precisely an operatic disaster it would seem to exhibit the quality we have found in them – perhaps in a supreme form. The great Albert Einstein was among other things a brilliant amateur violinist – he led a very fine amateur/quasi-professional quartet at Harvard for many years. One evening he simply couldn't get it right. (What violinist doesn't know the feeling?) It was, of course, one of those 'easy' early Haydn quartets. After Einstein failed to get the second movement started correctly for the fourth time, the cellist looked up at him in despair and said 'The problem with you, Albert, is that you simply can't count.'

LA BOHÈME
London Opera Centre

The soprano Linda Esther Gray recalls that 'I was the very last student to be trained at the old Opera Centre in the East End of London. The only time I've ever seen a singer fall asleep on stage was in an Opera Centre production.

'The poor tenor in *La Bohème* was unwell and had filled himself up to the eyeballs with Valium. I was playing Mimi and was dying in Act IV. Musetta produced an expensive muff to keep me warm on my deathbed and I asked if she had bought it. The tenor was supposed to sing 'I did' but as he (apparently sunk in despair over the foot of the bed) was sound asleep, Musetta sang the line instead of him. That's what I call presence of mind.'

THEA MUSGRAVE
London Opera Centre, 1961

I was assisting that most meticulous of directors, Anthony Besch, in one of the first performances of this excellent work, conducted by the composer. The plot revolves almost entirely around the presence of a corpse in bed – he has just died before the opera begins – and concerns the reactions of his family and friends. Therefore it is of paramount importance that there should actually *be* a corpse in the bed. The props department had made a really excellent and realistic dummy. Anthony, quite rightly, trusted neither me nor anyone else to make certain that all was ready, and insisted on carrying the corpse on himself. However, in the flurry that precedes any opera performance, he forgot until the very last moment, and the curtain rose to reveal to the astonished audience an elegantly dinner-jacketed figure rushing across the stage clutching a very life-like body. After the intensely grim and funereal overture it did not strike quite the right note, not least because the opera is set in medieval Scotland.

DON CARLO
G. Verdi, Royal Opera House, Covent Garden, London, 1959

One of the most attractive and eye-catching features of this Visconti production was a real tennis match which took place in the second act, behind the central characters in the palace of the Queen of Spain. On the first night, at which I was present, it was an elegant Velazquez-like scene, with two extras batting a small tennis ball to and fro very slowly, not interfering with the main action. On the second night, however, the duty fell to two Royal Opera extras whose spare-time passion was tennis. Completely forgetting where they were or what they were doing, they started hitting the ball in real earnest. The match ended with a terrific forearm smash, which fortunately missed Boris Christoff, singing Philip II, by inches before landing in the orchestra pit.

PELLÉAS ET MÉLISANDE
Claude Debussy (date and locale unknown)

Debussy's *Pelléas et Mélisande* is fraught with dangers. So much can go wrong and nowhere so easily as in the scene in which Mélisande lets her hair down through the window under which her lover is waiting. Logistics dictate that the tress must be an implausible and usually ludicrous five or six feet long, and many opera enthusiasts treasure memories of the hair detaching itself at Pelléas' first impassioned grope, leaving him sheepishly holding a hank of yellowish nylon or tow with a suddenly shorn Mélisande looking furiously down at him. Elisabeth Söderström, however, once encountered a new and original hazard.

She was singing Mélisande and had been provided with a hideously ugly reddish-blonde plait, six feet long, which she duly lowered out of the window.

Unfortunately, the end of the plait landed straight in Pelléas's open mouth and his singing died away in a strangled gurgle. Relations after that were distinctly chilly, though he did his best to embrace her with the enthusiasm the part demanded.

LE NOZZE DI FIGARO
W. A. Mozart

Many a Count in *Le Nozze di Figaro* has found himself in most peculiar difficulties, greater even than those he has managed to create for himself. On one reported occasion he found that, owing to the fact that he had furnished the nuptial apartment for Figaro and Susanna particularly generously, the whole first act stage was cluttered with pieces of furniture covered with dust sheets. It so happened that this Count was a stand-in who had had little or no rehearsal before the production began. He therefore suddenly realized that when it came to the moment where he discovers Cherubino in hiding he had completely forgotten where to look. He rushed around, pulling sheet after sheet off piles and piles of furniture. Despite surreptitious and increasingly frantic attempts by Susanna and Basilio to point him in the right direction, he became so baffled that the only way the opera could proceed was for Cherubino voluntarily to jump out of hiding, thus giving a very strong reverse twist to the plot.

DER FREISCHÜTZ
Carl Maria von Weber, Hanover, 1960

I am most deeply grateful to Sir Ashley Clarke, former British Ambassador in Rome, and tireless organizer of Venice in Peril for the following story. Now with *Der Freischütz*, I hope the reader will agree, we enter the world of the absolutely incomprehensible. I have never met anybody who really knows what the opera is about. Silvio Varviso, despite having conducted the work many hundreds of times, tells me he doesn't know what it's about. August Everding, whose ravishing production was so much admired at Covent Garden, agrees that he too doesn't know what it is about. I certainly don't know. All I do know, or have ever gathered, is that the fatal seventh shot is not intended to hit Agathe – or rather it is, but it gets deflected on to Kaspar, which seems quite a good thing. Now, Sir Ashley assures me that on this particular occasion, however, it missed both of these characters and hit the tree, and that the stagehands, who didn't like that particular Max, dropped a dead hare out of the tree onto the stage. Poor shooting, if I may say so. To hit a hare which happened to be sitting in a tree with your *seventh* shot would disgrace even the proverbial Irishman who shot an arrow at the sky – and missed.

The MALEVOLENCE of
INANIMATE OBJECTS

TOSCA
Date and place unknown

It was a cut-price production of this most accident-prone of operas, with minimal sets. At the last moment the producer sent a young assistant out to find some cannon balls to give verisimilitude to the final scene. The assistant, a youth of imagination and initiative, returned in the nick of time with a job lot of rubber beach-balls. Hastily, they were painted black, equally hastily glued together to form a pile, and placed on the battlements, where they looked splendidly substantial. But, as Tosca rushed up the steps to take her fatal leap she managed to kick the pile. The glue must have been as cut-price as the beachballs, because the pile disintegrated and, liberated, the balls bounced down the steps, down the stage and soared over the orchestra pit to land in the stalls.

Over now to France, where again a thousand apologies to my French friends for failing to accord 'la belle France' the notoriety in this field of London or New York. One or two excuses – the first is that under the regime of M. Rolf Liebermann the Paris Opera has of course been transformed into one of the world's greatest houses; the second that almost all aspects of French opera which can be satirized have already been done by Berlioz in his memoirs. I can however proffer this from Mr Peter Ustinov . . .

DON QUIXOTE
Jules Massenet, L'Opéra, Paris

I quote his words, 'I had four windmills. The back one was working perfectly because it had a very small and therefore very intelligent man in it, thus this windmill was going around . . . The next one had a much larger and much denser man and it was turning very much more slowly. The third one had two men in it who did not get on politically, so the thing was quite uncertain, and the one in front had an electric motor which suddenly, on the first night, went into reverse so the wind was blowing in a different direction . . .

THE MAGIC FLUTE
W. A. Mozart, English National Opera, 1977

One Saturday night the baritone Niall Murray was playing Papageno in the English National Opera production of *The Magic Flute*, sung, of course, in English. At one point, Papageno and Tamino are waiting for a chariot to descend from the flies containing the three boy spirits who will tell them where to go next.

'But the chariot got stuck somewhere above our heads out of sight and there was a distinct shortage of spirits, apart from the faint off-stage piping of distressed trebles.

'"I think I can hear a chariot," I sang hopefully. "Yes, so can I," echoed Tamino loudly into the wings. Stagehands were fighting somewhere in the void above us to untangle the chariot but without result.

'In opera, you sometimes have to judge the moment when the audience is about to laugh and get in before them. "No wonder it's late," I told them. "That chariot runs on British Rail standard gauge."

'In the end, the stage manager decided that he must at least deliver the contents of the chariot. The magic flute fell from aloft. There were supposed to be some bells but they never materialized. But a bowl of fruit did. It fell with a crash on my head and sent me reeling.'

AIDA
Giuseppe Verdi, L'Opéra, Paris, 1971

Grace Bumbry, singing Amneris, was required to walk up an enormously impressive staircase – reminiscent of the order given by Robert de Montesquiou 'like the one in the Opera, only bigger' – when it slowly began to split down the middle into its two component parts, on each of which the singer had a foot. Only a balletic leap saved her from acute embarrassment, and indeed from being filleted like a kipper.

LA TRAVIATA
Giuseppe Verdi

The following story is told of Giuseppe di Stefano who was singing Alfredo. In the second act the libretto provides for him to hurl his card winnings at Violetta – symbol of payment for her past favours and the ultimate public insult. He reached into his breast pocket, then in gathering consternation into his trouser pockets and every other place where his dresser could have secreted the dummy notes. They were nowhere to be found, and he was forced to slap Violetta's face instead. She, quite unprepared for this assault, is said never to have forgiven him.

MOSES AND AARON
Arnold Schoenberg, Deutsch Oper am Rhein, Cologne, 1962

This production was already celebrated for Josef Greindl's performance as Moses. However on this particular night it ran into a problem. The orchestra was 'assisted' by a series of loudspeakers which both developed the orchestral sound and added a specially prepared stereophonic soundtrack. Unfortunately, by one of the laws we have begun to develop in opera disasters, the electronic system became inadvertently plugged in to the local US Air Force base. Thus, Moses found himself competing with a fantastic background of technical weather reports, snatches of Liberace and some of Elvis Presley's greatest hits.

It is true that Richard Strauss requires the tenor in *Intermezzo* to enter on skis – a treat all too infrequently offered to opera-goers, but at a Wexford Festival performance of Spontini's *La Vestale* the entire cast faced a kind of operatic Cresta Run.

LA VESTALE
Gasparo Spontini, Wexford Festival, 1980

*L*a Vestale is set in Imperial Rome, and for this Festival production the designer had reproduced the marble of the Roman Forum with flooring of shiny white plastic stretched over the steeply raked stage. The producer had considerately arranged for the plastic to be sprayed with a non-skid substance (the irreverent said it was lemonade), but on the final night it was forgotten. The tenor entered, top left, his feet shot from under him and he slid inartistically into the footlights. Struggling up, he managed to regain his feet and reach the comparative safety of the central altar, to which he clung, still singing. There he was joined by the High Priestess, who had managed to aim her skid more accurately. When the time came for the soprano – the Vestal of the title – to enter, she had been forewarned and stepped on exceedingly cautiously. She embarked on her big aria, and then realized that she was unable to move from the spot. Without stopping singing, she stepped into the wings, removed her shoes and returned. This only made matters worse, and she vanished a second time, to re-appear without her tights. The superior adhesive qualities of bare feet triumphed and she was

able to join the central group without loss of dignity. However, when the chorus – a crowd of priests, citizens and soldiers – entered, they had for some reason not taken in what was happening and one by one shot gloriously down the stage to join their colleagues in a struggling heap at the footlights.

DIE FLEDERMAUS
*Johann Strauss, Deutsche Oper am Rhein,
Cologne, 1962*

It was one of those glittering, Christmassy carnival productions and the whole of West German society was present. The director had decided, as usual (and quite rightly too) to have a few extra entertainments for the guests at Prince Orlovsky's party. On this occasion there was to be a piano recital, which inevitably involved the appearance of a piano on the stage. The action of the opera stopped and stagehands, suitably dressed as flunkeys, brought the piano in on wheels. Perhaps they pushed too hard, perhaps some officious person had over-oiled the ball-bearings to stop them squeaking and confusing the audience with untimely bat-noises, but whatever the cause, the piano became hopelessly out of control on the steeply-raked stage and it ran straight down, gathering speed as it went, and fell into the orchestra pit. Luckily it seems that the players saw it coming and scrambled for safety so the damage was restricted to two flattened tubas and one very dead Bechstein Grand.

The Ultimate Disaster

INDEX

128